ARE YOU
SMARTER THAN A
SCIENTIST?

NOTICE THE SIMILARITIES BETWEEN THE
'EXTINCT DINOSAURS' AND TODAY'S ANIMALS

E D W A R D   T A Y L O R

ISBN: 978-1-4834-5382-8 (sc)
ISBN: 978-1-4834-5383-5 (e)

Because of the dynamic nature of the Internet, any web addresses or links contained in
this book may have changed since publication and may no longer be valid. The views
expressed in this work are solely those of the author and do not necessarily reflect the
views of the publisher, and the publisher hereby disclaims any responsibility for them.

Any people depicted in stock imagery provided by Thinkstock are models,
and such images are being used for illustrative purposes only.
Certain stock imagery © Thinkstock.

Lulu Publishing Services rev. date: 07/29/2016

Contents

 # Introduction

The sun; at times worshipped as a God, known as the giver of life without which Earth would be a frozen ball of ice. Creator of night and day on Earth, even its secondary or reflected light is enough to power, to light up the face of the moon. The sun has always been a source of awe and wonder and from the very beginning of intelligent life the question has been; what powers the sun? For the first time the truth about the sun, the understanding of the sun is, in these pages, finally explained.

Here also are three currently accepted scientific theories sent to the garbage bin of wrong theories where they belong.

CHAPTER 1

OUR SUN THE IMPOSSIBLE BALL OF GAS

First the currently accepted, currently taught and soon to be proven wrong theory of the sun; *the sun is internally fuelled by hydrogen that will run out in roughly five billion years at which time the sun, as it runs out of energy internally will expand into the red giant stage, eventually the outer layers will expand into space leaving a white dwarf. After the sun cools down completely a black dwarf cinder will remain.* This is the mistaken belief of the life and death of our sun, and other similar stars, based on the current false understanding that our sun is internally fuelled by hydrogen; even though according to the known laws of physics this is an impossibility to which astronomers reply that the physics of the sun and other stars are not the same as the physics of Earth. In reality if you know and understand the physics of the Earth than you know and understand the physics of the sun, stars and of the very universe itself for the physics of Earth is the same as that of the universe and of everything within it! Therefore when scientists ignore their mistakes that go against the known laws of physics they are entering the realms of impossibility and imagination. The rules of physics in regards to gravity are the same on Earth as they are in the rest of the universe. The only place gravity acts differently is in the mistaken minds of today's scientists.

1

The theory of the sun composed of hydrogen gas is not only wrong but also impossible as I will show how this not only appears wrong to anyone who knows anything about engines, motors or chemical equations but it is also impossible by the known laws of physics which today's astrophysicists and astronomers completely ignore. This results in a one plus one equals three mistake that astronomers and astrophysicists are making concerning the sun and it is this major mistake that is being completely ignored as they go ahead with their crazy belief that the sun is made of and fueled by hydrogen! Again; not only wrong but impossibly wrong!

Astronomers and astronomy that ignores the known laws of physics is astronomy that has no basis in truth. Current astronomy ignores the physical impossibility of the sun made of and burning hydrogen as its internal fuel. It will quickly be seen that this simple yet basic mistake is responsible for further mistakes in all of astronomy till in the end all of current astronomy is nothing but false theories and major mistakes. Today's astronomy is nothing but a giant house of cards ready to fall with the revelation of one simple truth; following is that simple truth!

First the background on this impossible theory of the sun and its spawning of further more impossible theories and fictional scenarios. See if you can spot the mistake that scientists have overlooked.

Our sun is theorized to have formed from a huge primordial cloud of dust, rocks and gases. In the center of this cloud where the dust, rock and gases were thickest, a weak gravity formed as all objects of mass contain a gravitational force as explained by Newton. This weak gravity further compressed the already thickest part of this primordial cloud such that more mass from the surrounding area of cloud was pulled into the central part of this cloud. As the mass in the center continued to increase so did the force of gravity as they are related on a one to one basis such that as mass increases in an object or an area of space so does the gravitational force of that object or area of space also increase. Astronomers then theorize that in this increasingly denser cloud of matter that as the gravity increases the hydrogen gases become denser and thicker and continue to grow larger and larger in the very center of this cloud while the rocks and dust are expelled to eventually form the sun which is now composed of a huge ball of dense, possibly liquid, hydrogen gas!

The one plus one equals three mistake is there and clearly stated in the previous paragraph on the theorized creation of the sun, see if you can spot this mistake as astronomers and astrophysicists have failed to do. If you see it than you are smarter than an astronomer or astrophysicist!

Astronomers do a great job of masking the truth as for a long while I read their theory and believed it; after all they are the scientists who have degrees and everything. Who am I, one of the ignorant masses a lay person after all to say that astronomers and astrophysicists are wrong. Even the scientists themselves still don't see, realize or admit their mistake. Yet it didn't seem to ring true and for a long time this theory bothered me until I finally realized what was so impossibly wrong about it, but first some further history and possible clues that also points to the mistaken theory on the sun and all stars predominately composed of hydrogen as impossibly wrong.

Hydrogen has a known mass and even in its denser forms this mass can be calculated. Sometime after the theory of the sun and all stars primarily composed of hydrogen was put forward calculations were done by other scientists that showed that the known actual force of gravity in the solar system and even the universe was not possible given the theoretical masses of the stars as dense balls of hydrogen. The mass to gravity ratio wasn't one to one like it should be, in other words given the known force of gravity in the solar system and the universe there should be larger amounts of mass or bodies of matter in the solar system and the universe to create this known strength of gravity but the problem quickly became apparent that there wasn't enough mass in the known solar system or the universe if the stars were actually created of hydrogen. As a result of these mass to gravity calculations there is 'missing mass' in the solar system and the universe that scientists have been trying to find and instead of realizing that their theory on the composition of the sun and all stars are wrong and impossibly wrong, astronomers and astrophysicists instead barreled forward and invented other wrong theories to explain the 'missing mass' such that they now believe that there is matter in space that is unseen by normal methods but must be there because of the 'missing mass'! This theorized matter that must be there and was solely invented by astronomers and astrophysicists to satisfy the 'missing mass' problem is called 'dark matter' and further because these same scientists know there must be 'dark matter' there must also be 'dark energy'! Intensive studies and research projects, costing untold tax payer dollars, have been launched in the search for the non-existent 'dark matter' and its further non-existent component 'dark energy'; after all the astronomers and astrophysicists know it must be there because their theory on the sun can't be wrong! They are the experts after all and they don't hesitate to tell us that we are only ignorant lay people!

For a long time I believed as they said, there must be some 'missing mass' somewhere yet their theory on the sun continued to bother me. Finally after reading about the arrangement of the Earth I realized why the theory of the sun was not only wrong but impossible! It has long been known that the Earth is arranged by density, the denser matter congregates in the center of the Earth while less dense matter sits on top of this. The Earth's oceans and even the atmosphere of Earth are all arranged by density. This means that Earth's gravity arranged matter within itself by density. Simply put; the Earth is composed of lessening rings of density from the Earth's densest central core to its surface and including the least dense atmosphere. Earth's gravity arranged matter by density or simply stated; **gravity arranges matter by density.**

Following is a simple visual experiment to prove and show how the Earth is arranged by density and a major clue as to why the theory on the sun is impossible! Imagine an empty five gallon bucket or container, the bucket is not actually empty on our planet Earth as it is filled with air.

Pour water into this bucket and the water displaces the air and settles on the bottom of the bucket towards Earth's center of gravity or towards the center of the Earth. Next pour sand into this bucket of water and you will notice that the sand settles to the bottom of the bucket displacing the water. Next put some rocks in this bucket of sand, water and air and you will notice that the rocks also settle to the bottom of the bucket towards the center of the Earth. If you were to add lead or other more dense materials to this bucket and shook the bucket you would then find that the denser lead settled to the bottom with rocks on top of the lead and the sand, water and air would have been displaced upwards to make room for the heavier, denser rocks and lead.

What does this prove? It proves that gravity; any gravity arranges matter by its density or mass such that the heavier objects settle towards the center of gravity while the lighter masses such as gases are displaced outwards and upwards further away from the center of gravity.

With this clue, this visual aid of the bucket let's take another look at the current scientifically accepted theory on the creation of the sun and see if you the ignorant lay person are smarter than an astronomer or astrophysicist. If you can spot the one plus one equals three mistake of physics you have shown yourself, the student, to be smarter than the so-called master or professor of astronomy! The student has become the master!

Our sun is theorized to have formed from a huge primordial cloud of dust, rocks and gases. In the center of this cloud where the dust, rock and gases were thickest, a weak gravity formed as all objects of mass contain a gravitational force as explained by Newton. They then theorize that in this increasingly denser cloud of matter that as the gravity increases the hydrogen gases become denser and thicker and continue to grow larger and larger in the very center of this cloud <u>while the rocks and dust are expelled to eventually form the sun which is now composed of a huge ball of dense, possibly liquid, hydrogen gas</u>!

The previous paragraph in shortened form contains the unmistakable error on the theory of the creation of the sun; the impossible ignoring the impossible twisting by scientists of known laws of physics, the one plus one equals three error. Astronomers are totally ignoring the laws of physics concerning the gravitational displacement of matter in relation to its density or mass and as known and shown with the Earth and as known and shown with the previous bucket example.

This is the specific spot where the theory on the sun takes a complete U-turn and totally goes against the laws of physics. The impossible even crazy part of the theory is this; *the hydrogen gases then coalesced or concentrated in the center of the sun, as gravity continued to increase more rocks and dust are displaced as more hydrogen gas is pulled into the center of the sun until gravity becomes so intense that nuclear fusion eventually ignites the dense hydrogen in the center of the sun. This is how our modern day sun was born.* Impossible and even stupidly impossible, gravity will not nor cannot pull hydrogen or any lighter gases towards the center of gravity over heavier dust, rocks or any other heavier matter as proven with the previous bucket example! What happened is that as gravity increased in the primordial cloud of dust, rocks and gases, the heavier dust and rocks coalesced into the center of the young sun displacing the lighter gases such as hydrogen outwards, just as we see happening today with the sun currently expelling hydrogen as an exhaust gas. As more dust and rocks were pulled in by the increasing gravity of the young sun the inner denser and heavier matter in the center of the sun started to heat up and eventually melted which then caused further displacement of lighter molten metals outwards and upwards leaving the heavier denser metals in the core of the sun. Any and all hydrogen or light gases released from chemical bonds to other elements are then discharged or forcibly displaced by gravity in an outgoing stream or exhaust of hydrogen and other light elements such as we see today and which is called the solar wind but could be called the solar exhaust stream.

* (The paragraphs in italics on the creation of the sun are in my words and not quoted.)

The sun was created from a huge cloud of gas, dust and rocks as theorized but the end result as clearly shown by the laws of physics is a super-dense solid body, the densest, largest body in our Solar System! Gravity arranged the matter in the sun by its density, similar to the bucket example and the Earth itself both of which are clear and simple examples that show the workings of the natural laws of physics concerning gravity and the displacement of matter by density. This clearly shows the actual workings of a gravitational force on matter and also that the physics of the sun and all stars is the same as the natural laws of physics on Earth. Gravity arranges matter by density on Earth the same as it does in the sun and all stars, planets and moons!

In conclusion; the fact (not theory) is that the sun is composed of heavier, denser matter such as lead and possibly even heavier materials. This then solves the 'missing mass' problem as there is no nor ever was any 'missing mass' only wrong theory on the creation of the sun. Therefore there is no 'dark matter' or 'dark energy' only mistaken theory. The simple truth is that the sun and all stars are composed of super dense matter.

The planet Jupiter is also thought by scientists to be mainly composed of hydrogen in liquid form. This is also impossible as any free hydrogen will be displaced outwards and upwards on Jupiter as well as on the sun and as on Earth as gravity displaces the lighter elements outwards from the center of gravity. It is highly unlikely that any free hydrogen or hydrogen not bonded to other elements will be found in any large quantity on any astronomical body of matter containing some strength of gravity other than in cloud formations of hydrogen gas on the edges of solar systems, galaxies and universes.

This also means that hydrogen is not the most abundant element of the universe as it is not the major component of any stars (even though scientists still believe this to be so today), but in fact hydrogen is one of the less common elements in the universe!

There have been missions recently undertaken by NASA with the intention of studying the sun in order to verify its makeup. Radar imaging of the sun was recently done by the SOHO satellite mission. The results of this radar imaging mission clearly showed that the sun was an immense solid body. Some of the popular magazines even ran articles on the newly discovered data concerning the dense solid sun. The scientific response to this new data was complete silence and total ignoring of the newly found facts on the solid seeming sun. Even though recent radar imaging shows that the sun is not composed of liquid hydrogen but rather is a dense solid astronomers totally ignored newly discovered scientific facts and observations. This because astronomers already know that the sun is composed of hydrogen, all the books say so, all the astronomers say so and all the students are taught so. Therefore any factual evidence to the contrary, even though the evidence explains the 'missing mass' problem must be false.

The wrong theory; namely that the sun is composed of hydrogen gas was accepted because no other theory of the time seemed to make any sense, while the discovery of the hydrogen bomb around the time of this theory seemed to confirm that the sun burned hydrogen similar to the newly discovered fusion of hydrogen in the hydrogen bomb. Even though problems arose with the sun composed of hydrogen such as the 'missing mass' problem and others all the problems were ignored and the theory gained acceptance amongst the scientists of the day until it is now considered the truth even though the 'missing mass' problem and others still can't be adequately explained. This then is the simple way to tell if a theory is false or true; if it creates more problems than it solves than it is most likely false, while the right theory will not only explain facts and observation it will open up new insights as well.

Let's take a look at the current theory of the sun composed of hydrogen for the likelihood of its truth or falseness.

1. 'Missing mass' problem yet to be adequately explained. Creation of new theories out of thin air such as hidden 'dark matter' and 'dark energy' that has to be there to explain the 'missing mass' problem!

2. Extremely high temperature area in outer 'atmosphere' of the sun that has yet to be adequately explained. Current theory holds that temperatures should rise towards the center of the sun where fusion of hydrogen is supposedly taking place, instead extremely high temperatures exist in the outer atmosphere of the sun and decrease towards the surface.

3. Large amounts of hydrogen discharged continuously from the sun that seems to be the exhaust but scientists avow is still the fuel because the sun supposedly contains large amounts of hydrogen within itself.

4. The most important overlooked mistake is that hydrogen pulled in by an increasing strength of gravity defies or goes against the known laws of physics as shown with the bucket example which clearly shows that gravity pulls in denser matter while displacing lighter gases such as hydrogen outwards, to which the usual scientific reply is that the physics of the sun is different than the physics of the Earth! What a load of crap! The physics of the Earth, sun and all bodies is the same throughout the universe. Gravity works the same on Earth as on the sun.

5. Recent, totally ignored by astronomers, radar imaging of the sun by the SOHO mission show that the sun is a dense solid not a ball of hydrogen gas or liquid but a dense solid body.

Let's now take a look at the new facts presented in this book that explains that the sun is composed of a super dense solid for its truth or falseness.

1. The 'missing mass' problem is solved as there is no 'missing mass' only wrong theory, with the understanding that the sun and all stars are composed of super dense matter the 'missing mass' problem no longer exists. The 'missing mass' is in the stars themselves! 'Dark matter' and 'dark energy' can go back into the imaginations of astronomers.

2. The sun is externally fuelled as matter is pulled into the sun on a continuous basis and melted and possibly undergoing fusion in the outer atmosphere of the sun due to its immense gravitational pressure. It is from this extremely hot outer atmosphere that hydrogen and all lighter gases and elements are discharged back into space while the heavier breakdown elements fall to the surface of the continually growing sun.

3. Chemical, heat and possibly fusion breakdowns of all matter pulled into the sun results in the continuous discharge of hydrogen by the sun along with large volumes of heat and light in the solar wind or exhaust of the sun.

4. The sun composed of super dense material fits the known laws of physics concerning an increasing strength of gravity in which denser material is pulled towards the center while lighter density material is expelled upwards and outwards just as in the solar wind composed of hydrogen and helium exhaust gases. This also proves that the physics of the sun and space are not different than that of Earths but are exactly the same.

5. This theory explains the recent SOHO mission on the sun in which radar imaging of the sun showed that it was a solid body! This is a fact that scientific proponents of the old theory completely ignore.

The new fact; that the sun is a super dense solid, explains away the old problems while opening up new areas of research. Therefore the old theory is definitely wrong for the above listed reasons and because it created more problems than it solved while the new theory/fact fits all current observations and known facts on the sun as well as the laws of physics. Therefore the new theory is fact while the old theory is discarded; after astronomers take their blinders off and new research is done with the new realization and eventual acceptance that the sun is a dense solid other upcoming facts will show the truth of this as well such as the following simple explanation of sunspots that are currently a mystery to today's scientists.

CHAPTER 2

SUNSPOTS AND THE SUNS FUEL STREAM

The new fact; that the sun is composed of a super dense solid explains away previous problems while opening new areas to investigate such as what is the actual fuel of the sun that is being burnt in the high temperature outer 'atmosphere' of the sun?

The new realization that the sun is externally fuelled from space and that this continuous stream of fuel is burnt in the outer atmosphere of the sun also explains sunspots on the surface or face of the sun. For those unaware of what sunspots are here is a brief explanation; Dark spots of varying sizes float across the bright face of the sun in what seem to be repeating patterns based on an eleven year cycle of the largest sunspot. These dark spots are areas of high energy releases around their edges but seem to be quiet in their centers. Current scientific thought is that magnetic lines of force build up within the sun and force an escape of the suns gravity through sunspots, taking large amounts of energy with them. Therefore it is thought by some scientists that a buildup of magnetic forces within the sun is responsible for the creation of sunspots on the face of the sun.

Here is the true and simple explanation of sunspots; the eleven year cycle of sunspots and the realization that the sun is externally fuelled simply and easily explains the existence of sunspots on the face of the sun; sunspots are simply planetary eclipses on the face of the sun! Jupiter the largest planet coincidentally has roughly an eleven year orbit around the sun and it is this same planet Jupiter that is responsible for the largest sunspot on the face of the sun! Scientists mistakenly searched for clues to sunspots within the sun when the truth lain external to the sun in that the orbits of the planets and moons roughly correspond to the known cycles of sunspots. (Future studies of the specific relationship of each sunspot to its corresponding planetary body will verify this newly discovered fact.) Astronomers were simply looking in the wrong direction!

Sunspots on the face of our sun represent planets and moons within our own Solar System; it may be possible to detect sunspots on other stars in order to detect hidden planets and moons around other star systems

The sun's fuel is pulled into the sun on a continuous basis by the sun's strength of gravity; this fuel stream passes through the length and breadth of the solar system past all of the planets, moons and asteroid belts in the solar system, this fuel stream comes in a 360 degree or spherical sweep of space. Similar to a small whirlpool and the same in shape as that seen in pictures of galaxies for the galaxies also have their fuel streams as well! It may have two or more arms as well but this is something for future research.

The planets and to a lesser degree the moons intercept some of this fuel that comes within reach of their respective gravitational fields. This leaves a hole, gap or tunnel of empty fuel in the sun's incoming fuel supply which in turn results in a dark sunspot on the face of the sun. Sunspots are simply planetary and planetary moons eclipses on the face of the sun caused by the respective planets and even the moons intercepting and emptying space of the fuel around them, basically creating a tunnel empty of fuel.

Coincidentally at the solar maximum of the eleven year sunspot cycle when sunspots are the most active there are up to 200 sunspots on the face of the sun while at the solar minimum none are visible but if you count the moons, dwarf planets and planets of the solar system you find also that there are roughly 200 bodies in our system! Positive proof that each planet and the many planetary moons are simply a reflection an eclipse on the face of the sun! Further research as to which planet matches which sunspot will bear this out and will also show if any hidden bodies exist in our system!

This is also the simple explanation to the scientific mystery of why the planet Jupiter gives off more energy than it receives. The planet Jupiter is too far from the sun to absorb much of the solar output yet it continually emits a steady output of heat energy from an unknown source!

The simple answer is that Jupiter, the largest planet in the Solar System intercepts the largest amount of matter from the sun's incoming fuel stream as it goes by and through the Solar System. Jupiter, as it continually absorbs matter from the sun's incoming fuel stream is constantly growing as it sucks up matter from outer space and emits heat energy as an end result of its continual growth. (A mystery simply solved when the right theory is proven!)

Jupiter and the rest of the planets and even the moons of our Solar System are the reason for sunspots on the face of the sun. The planets and moons are eclipses or reflections of themselves that result in dark areas absent of fuel on the surface of the sun.

A simple way to picture the sun's incoming fuel stream and resulting sunspots is to imagine a river flowing with rocks in it. The river's flow varies with the seasons as does the sun's incoming fuel stream resulting in less or more of a solar output. (The sun's seasons are far longer and can be seen in the record of the sun's output through the years.) The rocks in the stream are the planets and moons; as the water or incoming fuel of the sun flows around the rocks or planets the fuel is bunched up around the edges resulting in increased energy outbursts around the sunspots edges on the surface of the sun and a total absence of fuel in the sunspots center as a result of the planets interception of fuel. This is the simple explanation of sunspots that has posed a mystery to astronomers for many years.

The bunching up of fuel around the edges of a planets gravitational field results in solar flares of excessive energy on the face of the sun around the edges of the sunspots; Similar to the foaming of water over a rock in a fast moving stream of water. Solar prominences are also simply bunching up of excess fuel in the sun's incoming fuel stream resulting in the igniting out in space of this excess fuel similar to the ignition of thrown gasoline!

The eleven year sunspot cycle is caused by the planet Jupiter as it is the only planet large enough and close enough to the sun to affect the sun's actual orbit and spin. Jupiter's orbit is slightly off of the sun's true axis of rotation therefore it pulls the sun slightly off of its orbit and spin and as it does so it affects the sun's location in the larger galactic fuel stream. This in turn affects the amount of fuel the sun is able to pull into itself accounting for the solar maximums and minimums in which the sun burns brightly or dimly!

The sun's fuel stream is simply dust and small rocks intercepted or swept from space by the sun's massive gravitational field that extends past the outermost planet or asteroid belt as the sun moves through its orbit in space. Similar to a giant well or vortex in space that pulls all matter within it in a slow spiral towards the sun in the center where the heavier matter is burned up and added to the sun itself while the lighter end products such as hydrogen, helium and heat are expelled outwards in a continuous process.

The simple explanation of sunspots also proves that the sun is externally fuelled and not internally fuelled by hydrogen. Hydrogen is more plainly shown to be an exhaust gas of the sun, while dust, micrometeorites and small rocks from space are shown to be the continuous fuel source of the sun as is the occasional comet.

The explanation of the sun's external fuel stream and the interception of this fuel stream by the planets and moons also show that not only Jupiter and the sun are increasing in size but all the planets are growing in size as they accumulate extra matter from space as they intercept it from the sun's fuel stream. In other words all the planets, moons and the sun itself are constantly growing in size as their respective gravities pull in matter or mass from space. The amount of matter pulled in by each planet or moon depends on its gravitational strength, its overall size and its location in relation to the sun as those planets closer to the sun receive a more concentrated amount of fuel compared to those planets further from the sun; also the inner planets will occasionally hit an area of space already swept clean of fuel by the outer planets as well as the occasional bunching of fuel caused by the outer planets.

The simple answer to the question of whether the Earth is growing, decreasing or staying the same in size is that the Earth is without a doubt constantly growing in size and mass as it continually pulls in matter from space daily, hourly and minutely. Likewise for all of the bodies of the Solar System, as well as all the stars in the universe, each is continually growing in size with the sun at the center of our system growing the fastest. Nothing in this universe stays the same as the dust of time covers all.

Astronomers made the simple mistake of looking for answers internally on the sun when the simple truth was external or outwards from the sun; they were so convinced of the sun's internal fires that they were blind to the truth!

CHAPTER 3

EARTH'S INCREASING GRAVITY

Has Earth's gravity remained the same? This question has recently been asked in the halls of science and scientists are uncomfortable with the question and more so with the logical answer. Therefore science and scientists have again been trying to suppress and minimize the truth; as the written books authored, preached as fact and sold by these same scientists claim that the size of Earth has largely remained the same throughout its long history.

Science has long known that all matter has weight or mass and that the Earth's mass or weight could be calculated and is known. The question remains is this calculated mass of the Earth constant. Let's look at the known facts.

Meteor showers on Earth are a regular occurrence and bring matter from space to Earth. All matter has mass or weight; therefore meteor showers add mass or weight to the Earth. Scientists say that this is a miniscule amount in comparison to the size of the Earth and that this hardly affects Earth's gravity, yet all mass added to the Earth, however miniscule adds a miniscule amount of gravity to the Earth as an objects gravity is directly related to its mass. Therefore as the Earth's mass increases so does its gravity! This is a known physical fact or constant yet scientists are reluctant to face the truth as it means admitting they are wrong as well as admitting their books are wrong and their teaching of students is also wrong!

Another factor in Earth's changing gravity also being suppressed is the fact that Earth itself regularly receives from space a dusting of matter on a daily, hourly, minutely basis. If you garden or even if you don't you might have noticed an occasional dusting of matter on the leaves of plants on a quiet morning; this dusting is the result of micrometeorites or space dust that is constantly pulled to the Earth from space. Some of this dust is arguably windblown erosion but a large amount of this dusting seen on plants comes from space and is deposited over the face of the Earth including the oceans. The question on this is how much matter is being pulled in from space. Some estimates range from thousands of tons daily over the whole face of the Earth to just a few tons daily. The problem is that the amount is variable depending on how dirty the area of space is that the Earth is currently passing through, yet this dusting is evident in the layering or covering over of past extinct civilizations in dirt several feet thick at times. Again some of this dirt comes from windblown erosion yet a large amount comes from space. Regardless of the scientifically agreed upon amount this tonnage of dusting from space adds mass to the Earth on a daily basis which in turn increases Earth's gravity on a daily basis.

Large meteors have occasionally hit the Earth over its long history as evidenced by the occasional large craters left behind after a large meteor impact.

If you were to ask scientists about large meteor impacts on the Earth and their effects on Earth's gravity and past extinctions you would get an answer something like this; (following is a hypothetical conversation with a scientist) Question; what happened to the dinosaurs? (Hypothetical answer ;) We believe that the dinosaurs were wiped out in a mass extinction by a massive meteor from space as multiple craters around the Earth show that

Earth has been occasionally hit over the millennia. We are currently unsure as to which meteor crater was responsible for the dinosaurs' extinction. (Hypothetical question;) Has Earth's gravity changed? (Hypothetical answer;) We currently believe that Earth's size and gravity have largely remained the same over the millennia.

Even though scientists will openly acknowledge that Earth has been hit by large meteors in the past some several miles wide as shown by craters on the face of the Earth and not even counting those that hit the oceans or ice caps and are currently unseen, they will openly deny that Earth's gravity is changing or has changed as it is an accepted teaching and belief of current scientists that Earth's gravity has largely remained the same; this even while they acknowledge that large meteorites/small planetoids have been added to Earth's mass and gravity. Talk about being blind to the truth! Further, scientists will acknowledge that because of Earth's weathering effects and oceans many physical signs of meteors hitting Earth are already erased plus if you look at the surrounding dead planets and moons abundant meteor cratering exists on all of them. This means that Earth itself was also heavily bombarded by meteors from space but the evidence for this has been erased by the weathering effects on the face of the Earth.

To sum it all up;

1. We have large meteors/small planetoids occasionally colliding with the Earth.
2. The yearly meteor showers adding mass to the Earth.
3. The daily dusting of micrometeorites amounting to some tons of matter also added to the Earth.

All mass has gravity while increasing mass increases gravity. The Earth's mass increases daily therefore Earth's gravity increases daily, even if it is in miniscule amounts it is still gradually increasing. Yet science and more specifically scientists still refuse to acknowledge this fact as it would mean admitting that they are wrong plus they would have to rewrite the books on Earth's increasing gravity and the increasing mass of the Earth, the same books that they wrote and authored and profit from! This would also force them to revise and question other theories based on the false theory and false belief that the Earth and its gravity have largely stayed the same.

All planets, moons and stars are continually growing in mass and strength of gravity. The rates of growth vary depending on each bodies mass and location. It is an undisputable fact that Earth is growing in mass and strength of gravity. Those that refuse to acknowledge the facts and truths are simply protecting their profits and reputations.

CHAPTER 4

YESTERDAY'S 'DINOSAUR' TODAY'S ANIMALS

When it is understood that Earth's gravity is continuously increasing over time other problems and their solutions become apparent; such as what happens to life forms on an Earth with an increasing gravity? The simple, logical answer is that life forms gradually become smaller. It is this new found realization, that life forms on Earth will gradually become smaller over time as gravity increases that forces us to look anew at old theories; specifically the theory on animal and 'dinosaur' extinctions.

The question now becomes; knowing that increasing gravity on Earth will eventually cause a decrease in size of life forms on Earth, is there evidence in the past history of Earth of such decreases in animal size? The logical answer is of course a resounding 'yes' as multiple recorded extinction events show a gradual decrease in size of past life forms. Only entrenched scientists and so-called experts have yet to see the truth.

Currently accepted scientific theory holds that the 'dinosaurs' are extinct, that they died out millions of years ago, the so called proof of this is the simple fact that there are no super large 'dinosaurs' walking around on Earth today, therefore, logically they must be extinct!

The new found realization that Earth's gravity has been steadily increasing over time while life forms were steadily decreasing in size over time forces us to look anew at the question of 'dinosaur' extinctions. Of course the theory on 'dinosaur' extinction is wrong and again the true answer is simple when seen in its entirety.

In a small defense of the scientists behind the wrong theory of the 'dinosaur's' extinction it must be understood that all that scientists have to go on in regards to all theories regarding 'dinosaurs' comes only from the fossilized bones of these once great animals. These fossilized bones have no flesh left on them, no viable DNA (as of today no viable 'dinosaur' DNA has been found), no skin or blood and frequently the bones are mixed with other animal bones or simply missing altogether so that only a partial skeleton remains. It is from these meager findings that all theories on 'dinosaurs' have arisen from. This is something like trying to rebuild a whole machine from one or two parts that were found. In other words, it is easy to make mistakes in regards to the rebuilding of 'dinosaurs' in their entirety from the little that is found remaining of them, while it is also easy to make mistakes in regards to possible theories about the once living 'dinosaurs' with the meager remains found.

(This is the only defense that I will give to the wrong theories on 'dinosaurs' as the very name of 'dinosaurs' is wrong! This is why the word 'dinosaur' is enclosed by harsh marks ' ' throughout this book, the term itself is wrong as the 'dinosaurs' of yesterday are of course today's animals.)

The name 'dinosaurs' means large lizard as it was originally thought that the 'dinosaurs' were cold blooded as are todays lizards. This is still the belief of scientists today but it is important to remember that no blood has been found in the fossilized bones in which to base this currently accepted yet wrong theory. It is simply a theory that has become accepted as fact over time because the scientist who first proposed the cold blooded theory and coined the name 'dinosaur' already had an established reputation in the scientific community, basically his opinions became accepted as fact by the scientific community without the benefit of any facts to back up his musings and opinions. In other words even today there is no proof that the 'dinosaurs' were cold blooded yet this is still currently believed to be true and still preached today because no proof has been bought forward to prove otherwise while the scientific community have banded together and all agree that the original opinion of their now dead scientific brethren is the right one. Plus all the books written and authored by these very same now dead scientists have within them the statement that; *'dinosaurs' were cold blooded*, to which today's scientists point to and also claim that 'dinosaurs' are cold blooded. Talk about a flimsy basis for a theory! Basically scientists have come together in defense of their dead scientific brother's wrong opinions and further convinced the world that their collective and supposedly educated opinion is the right one. If one were to ask for the scientific proof of the 'dinosaurs' being cold blooded you would find that your question is either ignored or you are belittled for asking such a question. It is important to remember that there are no currently proven and indisputable facts to show whether 'dinosaurs' were cold-blooded or warm-blooded, as no fossilized bones have yet been found with any blood vessels or cells intact. Everything stated by scientists in regards to 'dinosaurs' is simply conjecture, theories and currently accepted opinions! (Until now with the realization that gravity made all life forms smaller!)

The wrong theory that 'dinosaurs' are extinct came about because of all the super large fossilized bones found of gigantic animals that once roamed the face of this Earth. The simple conclusion drawn from the bones is that because there are no super large animals roaming the Earth today they must all be extinct! This theory seemed logical on the face of it. Yet when you look at it from different angles, dig deeper and start asking questions the theory itself shows that it cannot be totally accurate.

Earth millions of years ago at the time of the 'dinosaurs' had hundreds of animal species of the super-large variety around the world and further hundreds of species of super-large plants, super-large trees and super-large sea life. In other words super-large was the norm of the time.

The theory on the 'dinosaurs' extinction is that some catastrophe, most likely a hit from space by a large asteroid, caused such damage to the Earth on impact that volcanoes were set off, quakes were felt and huge clouds of dust and ash were sent flying into Earth's atmosphere. These clouds of dust blocked out the sun's rays for several years such that a mini-ice age followed with very few plants able to grow. Therefore all of the super-large species dependent on plants or plant-eaters to live on died off or became totally extinct. Many super-large plants and trees also became extinct but Earth itself survived with nothing else changed, according to current scientific theory. Here-in lies the problem; if nothing else on Earth changed during the 'dinosaur' or super-large die-off and 'dinosaurs' lived for millions of years after first evolving into their super-large sizes, then why haven't super-large sizes evolved again the world over? At the very least the super-large plants and tree species whose seeds can lie dormant in the soil for many years should have quickly reappeared. There should now be the same super-large ferns and trees and other super-large plant life on Earth now as there was in the past. Even the animal life, after several millions of years having passed since the large asteroid hit the Earth that first caused the extinction event, should by now have again evolved into the super-large size. Yet this is not the case, in fact there is not one super-large species of plant, tree or animal alive today that comes close to the super-large size life forms of the 'dinosaur' age. Clearly something is amiss, something is not right. In spite of scientific claims to the contrary something on Earth has changed. Something on Earth is different from before the extinction event and after it. (As explained previously Earth's gravity has increased!)

Alligators, crocodiles, turtles and sharks are thought to be surviving species of the great 'dinosaur' extinction but of a mini species due to their smaller size. Even though the surviving species today are greatly similar in shape just far smaller in size they are classified as a separate species because the super large branch no longer exists. They're extinct after all! In other words it is believed that the smaller species alive today coexisted alongside the super large species that are similar in shape and form but that the super large species became extinct while the smaller species survived. So even though todays ferns, trees, alligators, crocs, turtles and sharks are exactly similar to their super large cousins they are not the same species but mini versions of the super large ones. The super large ones died out while the smaller versions, even though they are exactly the same other than size, the mini-species survived. This part of the theory seems farfetched but in all fairness it is possible for smaller and larger species that are similar in all other regards to coexist side by side as is currently the case on Earth. For example the lions, leopards, lynxes, bobcats and domesticated house cats are all similar but vary greatly in size. That said further proof will show that this is not actually the case with 'dinosaurs' and their so- called mini-relatives alive today. For instance why haven't the seeds of the super large trees and ferns survived if they were so plentiful in the extinct past while seeds from the mini-species survived? Seeds are very tough, can be covered over and hidden for multiple years to sprout anew when exposed to the right conditions. The super large trees and fern seeds should have survived along with the mini species alive today yet supposedly, according to the extinction theory they didn't because as we all know there are no super large species of anything alive on Earth today.

This then is the greater question; why are there no super large species alive on Earth today? If hundreds of super large species of animals and plants existed in ages past, why haven't any new species or even today's currently living species grown to the same super large size of these past animals and plants; after all with the complete death and extinction of the past super greats doesn't an opening exist in nature for other super large species to evolve into; and with the passage of millions of years since the time of the dinosaurs isn't it logical that at least one species of animal, fish, plant or tree should have evolved by now into a super large version?

The 'dinosaur' extinction question needs to be rephrased to; why hasn't nature again evolved super large species of plants or animals? It did so in the past in multiple cases as proven by the fossilized 'dinosaur' bones, fossils of giant ferns, trees and other plants. The simple logical answer is that something in nature or the natural world has changed such that the super-large size is no longer the norm.

Simply stated; something in nature has changed from the time of the dinosaurs till now. Therefore even though current scientific thinking assumes that the niche for super large species is still there in nature it is not. Something has changed so that today's elephants on land and whales in the seas are the largest possible animals allowed by nature today. Therefore even if by some miracle DNA of the 'dinosaurs' were found intact and were cloned into a living, breathing life form they would not become super large as they were in the past but would simply grow only as large as some of the animals today. This is the simple explanation as to why there are no super large animals or plants alive today, nature has changed so that it is no longer possible for the super greats to exist alive today!

This also explains another recurring problem with so-called 'dinosaur' extinction. Several independent scientists in the recent decades have done studies of dinosaur bones and with the help of computers and other technology have simulated the flesh around them. From these simulations they have been able to calculate the weight of the flesh and the weight of the 'dinosaurs' themselves and have been able to conclude that the immense weight of the 'dinosaurs' would not be able to be supported by the bones without breaking. In other words in today's world or in nature today 'dinosaurs' could not run or even walk without stumbling because if they did they would break a bone and eventually die either of their injuries or of eventual starvation. Several independent scientists have come to this same conclusion at different times over the past decades but these scientists results have been denied as inaccurate, wrong and just plain impossible by those scientists that refuse to believe these recently found facts. Even though the current scientific consensus on dinosaur extinction is accepted worldwide, faults and errors are showing up, to be denied and suppressed by those in power in the scientific world.

Ignored and suppressed by modern day scientists multiple scientific studies show that the 'dinosaurs' actual weight was too heavy for their bones, yet they not only existed in the past but thrived. Either the weight to bone studies done by several independent scientists all coming to the same conclusion are wrong or this points to the change in nature that no longer allows the super large to exist on Earth. What then could cause a size change in nature such that the super large animals of the past, the 'dinosaurs', could no longer exist on Earth as shown by multiple studies of weight to bone ratios? In order to answer this question we need to understand something else about the theory of 'dinosaur' extinction.

The theory of 'dinosaur' extinction is actually based on another theory or scientific opinion; this theory holds that the gravity of Earth has stayed largely the same over the millions of years of Earth's existence. If this theory is true, if Earth's gravity has stayed the same over millions of years of time then the multiple weight to bone studies of the 'dinosaurs' are wrong, the surviving species such as the alligators, sharks, trees and ferns are actually coexisting mini species and nature has an available niche for super large creatures that for one reason or another beyond our current level of understanding has yet to be filled even after the passage of several millions of years. Therefore any 'dinosaur' DNA found and cloned would result in super large animals again roaming the Earth.

The accepted theory for the cause of the 'dinosaurs' extinction is that a large meteor from space, several miles wide, hit the Earth causing massive destruction, with earthquakes, possibly volcanoes and huge clouds of debris and dust blocking out the sunlight causing a temporary cooling of Earth's climate. This temporary climate change caused massive food shortages killing off the remaining surviving 'dinosaurs'. A key phrase again ignored by scientists is that a giant meteor several miles wide hit the

Earth from space; in other words a small planetoid was added to Earth's mass which also increased Earth's gravity.

Earth's changing gravity needs to be acknowledged and accepted as true even if science and scientists lag behind, this can now be easily seen to be the reason for the change in nature or why the 'dinosaurs' of super large size are no longer allowed to attain there once great size. Earth's changing gravity is why the 'dinosaurs' weight to bone ratio testing done by various scientists proved that dinosaurs could not survive at there once great size without breaking a bone and dying. Earth's changing gravity is why the animals and plants of today are at a smaller size than those of the distant past. The trees, ferns, sharks, crocodiles, turtles and other surviving species thought to be mini-species coexisting with their now thought extinct super large cousins are in reality the super large species reduced to today's sizes according to today's gravity.

'Dinosaurs' could only be extinct if Earth's gravity has stayed the same and nature failed to fill the super large niche, but Earth's gravity has changed becoming stronger over the years to its present day level which is directly reflected in the size of today's animals, plants and all life forms including ourselves. Therefore 'dinosaurs' are not extinct they have merely shrunk in size to become today's animals. The proof, the simple undisputed proof is in the animals themselves.

A simple comparison of 'dinosaur' skeletons to today's animals shows the truth. The easiest to see is the skeleton of the long necked 'dinosaur' once called the brontosaurus, this 'dinosaur' is today's giraffe. Same long neck just greatly shrunk in size according to today's gravity but definitely not extinct. Remember skin color cannot be determined from fossilized bones only guessed at but the exact neck structure shows the truth. The armor plated tank-like 'dinosaur' called the triceratops is today's tough hide rhinoceros. The greatest predator 'dinosaur', the T-rex for short and its smaller relatives the Velociraptor along with still smaller predator versions shown on movies are still the greatest mammal predators feared on Earth as they are today's lions, tigers, bobcats, lynxes and domesticated cats. Same large jaws with large ripping teeth and claws, same large hind legs with small front legs but here is proven another mistake. Today's felines run on all fours, while the predators of the 'dinosaur' age supposedly ran on two legs. Does this prove an error and show that the predator 'dinosaurs' of yesterday are not the same as those of today? No but it does show that the bones of the T-rex are not assembled correctly. Remember the bones found of fossilized 'dinosaurs' are frequently incomplete or scattered and putting them together is like putting together a complicated jigsaw puzzle without a picture on the box to follow. Even today mistakes are still being realized as to the actual correct piecing together of 'dinosaur' bones; yet anyone that has a house cat or is familiar with the cat family can recognize the occasional posture of a cat in a sitting position with its front legs up while sitting on its larger hind legs. This is how the fossilized bones of many predator 'dinosaurs' were found in this sitting position; what happened is that prior to dying many of these predator 'dinosaurs' first relaxed in a sitting position before falling over onto their sides as death overcame them and as still frequently happens in the cat family today. Therefore the T-rex does not run as a computer simulated two legged predator but as a four legged predator; in other words it was far faster than is currently believed and is simply incorrectly assembled. So if you have a house cat you have a modern 'dinosaur' in your house or a mini-T-rex!

Supposedly the giant ground sloths of the Americas are also extinct but I believe they are today's badgers and wolverines again adjusted for size according to Earth's change of gravity. A further study of other supposedly extinct 'dinosaurs' compared to today's animals will most likely prove the further truth that they are one and the same. The animals to 'dinosaurs' that I have shown are only ones that are simple to see at a glance and easily recognizable even by children. The simple truth is that the so called extinct 'dinosaurs' of yesterday are simply todays mammals. The overlooked visual proof simply shows the truth. The actual number of species that went extinct are far less than what science currently believes.

The 'dinosaurs' were not cold blooded lizards but were warm blooded mammals that for the most part survived but in reduced size due to a change in Earth's gravity.

What is not commonly known is that there were supposedly multiple extinction events throughout Earth's history. Five major extinctions are thought to have occurred, the 'dinosaur' extinction being the latest major extinction event. As many as twenty extinction events, minor and major, are thought to have occurred with the latest believed to have occurred at the end of the last ice age around twelve thousand years ago. This last minor extinction event is called the mega fauna extinction and it supposedly happened after the 'dinosaur' extinction. This extinction saw the demise of the woolly mammoths and saber tooth tiger as well as multiple other species. If you take a look at the mega fauna species thought to be extinct by continent, you will see an extensive list of animals now thought to be gone. Each of these supposedly extinct species is slightly larger than those animals now alive. Yet if you read the mega fauna extinct species for Africa each one supposedly dead and gone is replaced by a slightly smaller version with only a few exceptions. (In other words the few exceptions are species that actually are extinct.) The giant gorilla is replaced by today's gorilla, something called a giraffid is replaced by today's smaller giraffe, and the giant hyena now extinct is replaced by today's hyena and so on and so on. Almost every larger species said to be extinct has a smaller surviving species that replaced it according to science and scientists. Again to clarify current scientific thinking; the larger extinct species are supposedly not the same as the current smaller species; they coexisted alongside one another while the larger species died out but the smaller survived. The simple truth is that contrary to current scientific thinking almost each animal thought to be extinct can be explained as the same species merely shrunk in size. Today's smaller tiger was the sabre toothed tiger which in turn was the T-rex. Each separate extinction event merely saw the stepped and gradual decrease in animal size as Earth's gravity increased. Just as you would logically expect it to when Earth is hit by a large meteor/planetoid from space.

Each large meteor strike of Earth caused extensive damage to Earth's ecosystem as the sun was blocked by dust, possible volcanic and earthquake action but each large meteor strike also increased Earth's gravity, causing an expected and corresponding decrease of animal size. Many animals died as the result of every meteor strike but many survived as they grew up in a slightly smaller form. Therefore very few species are actually extinct they are all today's surviving animals and plants. In reality 'dinosaurs' are not extinct they are simply today's animals just shrunk in size due to Earth's increasing gravity. In other words almost all of today's animals are descended from the non-extinct, not cold blooded, not related to lizards, animals mistakenly labeled as 'dinosaurs'! Therefore if you have a house cat or any pet you have a living descendant of a surviving 'dinosaur'!

Let's compare competing theories and their points on truth or falseness with the new knowledge and realization that Earth's gravity has been steadily increasing. The known and accepted facts by all are that multiple extinction or die-off events occurred on the face of the Earth over Earth's long past history in which each succeeding age is followed by smaller and smaller life forms in the plant and animal world.

The old, currently accepted by scientists theory is; 'dinosaurs' are extinct while the new theory is that 'dinosaurs' are simply today's animals; first the points of the old theory;

1. Scientists claim that over five billion species of all life forms on Earth of some twenty extinction events are now extinct with only their fossilized remains left to show that they once lived on this Earth.

2. Numerous large impact craters on the face of the Earth might be the trigger event behind the known mass extinctions. (This is not accepted as the cause by all of today's scientists.)

3. The scientific reasoning proving that 'dinosaurs' are extinct is that we don't see them on Earth today!

4. 'Dinosaurs' were cold blooded and related to today's lizards.

Now the new theory which claims that 'dinosaurs' and many of the billions of life forms supposedly extinct are still alive on Earth today, just shrunk in size due to increasing gravity.

1. With the logically proven increase in Earth's gravity throughout our past history it becomes apparent that all life forms on Earth have shrunk in size over time. Therefore most life forms thought to be extinct simply because we don't see their super large bodies walking the Earth or living on the face of the Earth are still alive today simply in smaller sizes.

2. The evidence of large meteors from space in the form of impact craters on the face of the Earth shows that Earth's mass and gravity have been increasing over time, while life form sizes decrease in size.

3. The simple reasoning of 'dinosaurs' are extinct because we don't see them isn't logical, evolution provided for thousands of super large sized creatures in the past, but not a single one now after the passage of millions of years of time since the 'dinosaurs' lived. The simple reason is that gravity has changed and continues to change.

4. The simple comparison of today's animals to supposedly extinct ones of the previous age shows that the same animals are still here just smaller in size. Today's animals are directly related to the 'dinosaurs'. Today's animals are warm blooded therefore their ancestors the 'dinosaurs' were also warm blooded.

This conclusively and logically proves that 'dinosaurs' are not extinct but are today's mammals and that Earth's gravity is steadily increasing and has not stayed the same. Two mistakes of today's currently accepted scientific views proven false; plus earlier proof that the sun is a dense solid explains three mistakes of today's scientific consensus or to state it correctly simply wrong scientific opinion.

CHAPTER 5

AMERICAS BROKEN BELIEF SYSTEM

Astronomers have made the mistake of assuming a theory is correct simply because the math is solved for a particular theory and adding further wrong theories on top of the original unproven theory. Math does not prove whether a theory is correct or not it only shows that a particular theory is mathematically possible. In the end astronomers have created a house of cards built on nothing but mistakes. Further astronomers have banded together in defense of their mistakes making their mutual ignorance the actual problem while they simply ignore or deny the real truth and factual observations.

Sometimes it is necessary to ignore current scientific thinking and theories, to think outside of the box. It is this thinking that allowed the Wright brothers to fly when science said it was impossible, that allowed Columbus to discover the new world when he realized that the world was not flat. Science and scientists need to be ignored when they denounce giant squid as myths from their comfortable armchairs while calling multiple ships' captains and sailor's factual sightings out in nature, out in the field, nothing but drunken stories; finally admitting that giant squids existed when a dead body of one washed ashore. Darwin did not come to his sweeping conclusions on evolution by studying previous scientists biased written opinions but by going physically to the Galapagos islands and studying the life forms there. Science and scientists need to be ignored when multiple people collect meteors seen to fall from space that are still warm only to be called ignorant peasants. Science and scientists again need to be ignored when they call 'dinosaurs' extinct and claim that Earth's gravity has stayed largely the same throughout history when the facts clearly prove otherwise.

Here is what will happen in the scientific world after this book is published; people will read this book and start to question the wrong scientific theories that scientists are still pushing as the truth. Some scientists will even read this book but even seeing the proven facts on why dinosaurs are today's mammals, why Earth's gravity is increasing and why the sun is a dense solid they will still deny and even denounce this book as full of lies, after all it is the scientists false reputations, prestige and money at stake. Many people will still cling to the words of the scientists, after all they are the so-called experts and the scientists themselves will even tell you that they are the experts. The scientists will tell you that this book has no merit as it is written by a non-scientist, one with no degree or scientific background and this part will be true but remember that in spite of no scientific background the Wright brothers proved that it was possible to fly, Columbus that the world wasn't flat. Plus if you look closely at most scientific breakthroughs you will see the hidden truth that the majority of new ideas came from outside of the scientific community, were vehemently denied by the scientific community and finally and reluctantly were accepted by the scientific community as fact. (Many non-scientists outside of the scientific community were given honorary doctorates after the facts of their ideas were accepted.) Established science is actually a deterrent to new discoveries and groundbreaking ideas as they resent any new thinking that might upset their status quo, their position and power. How much sooner might mankind have been flying if instead of saying that mankind was not meant to fly scientists might have said it may be possible to fly but the only way to find out was thru trial and error. There are many examples in recent history of accepted scientific beliefs or scientific dogma deterring further investigation and it is still happening today as this book attempts to show!

Science and the scientists behind today's science have a bad habit of taking an unproven theory as fact and further teaching unproven theories to students as facts. When an unproven theory is first presented and awards are given out for the novel idea the unproven theory becomes almost written in stone and impossible to disprove without multiple facts against it and even then some scientists still cling to the unproven theory as that is what they were taught as true. In other words todays accepted science is not all true just because the scientists behind it have won awards and are famous because of their ground breaking theories and these theories are now taught as facts in colleges around the world. Even the writing of popular books and movies by these same famous scientists does not prove their theories to be true only currently accepted. This book showcases several theories readily accepted by science, scientists and the world at large today that are simply wrong, stupidly wrong and downright impossible yet they are readily believed to be true today because the scientists behind them have won awards from their peers for their ideas; the greater public, not knowing otherwise, have accepted these wrong theories as fact. Even in today's science magazines and journals these wrong theories are currently being discussed as facts; even though multiple problems with these very same theories point to their falsehood. Instead of going back to the original wrong theory where the problems first crop up today's scientists forge ahead and propose further false theories to support the original wrong one. This is simply bad science.

Many new theories come from outside the scientific world or from non-scientists. This usually sparks vehement denial, ridicule and even outright suppression from the scientific community. If the new theory is finally accepted it is only after the entrenched scientists realize their mistakes yet no apologies are given while the person behind the new theory is accepted as one of their own with 'honorary' degrees given out. In this way it looks as if all new theories come from within the scientific community when in fact this is rarely the case. Most new theories come from without the scientific community, many are not accepted until decades later when new evidence comes out verifying the truth of the new theory, many times after the person coming out with the new theory is already dead.

Astronomers, paleontologists, geologists and other scientists have banded together in the total belief of their false thinking and beliefs and will not be told otherwise. This shows what the state of science is that we are listening to. Just like the story of the emperor with no clothes we are being told scientifically agreed upon lies by the scientific community and because they are all preaching the same thing who are we to say otherwise. Even knowing that the facts prove otherwise and that the laws of physics prove otherwise, who are we to say that the sun is a dense solid body, that Earth's gravity is increasing and that 'dinosaurs' are not extinct but are todays mammals? After all they have the degrees in science. Why don't they see the truth or the facts but instead totally ignore the laws of physics; what is going on here? The truth is that for today's scientists it isn't about the truth but about the power, the money and the prestige. The truth the actual physical proofs of nature and of the Earth, the truth behind the physics of the sun and space have become of secondary importance after power, money and prestige.

This shows that science and scientists themselves are the main stumbling block to new advances in knowledge. The Wright brothers did not listen to current scientific thought which held that 'if mankind was meant to fly he would have been born with wings'. Giant squid were frequently reported by ship's captains but until a dead giant squid washed up on shore they were dismissed as unfounded myths of drunken sailors! Meteors were thought to be impossible by the scientific community with papers written by leading couch scientists of the day denouncing their existence, causing museum curators to destroy their collections of meteorites. Giant dinosaur bones were thought at first to be nothing but a hoax and many were destroyed because of current scientific thinking until whole skeletons started showing up and someone started piecing them together. The scientific community is slow to change even when those outside the scientific community produce undisputable proof. Scientists denounce the non-scientists as ignorant crackpots even when the number of sightings and actual physical proofs show otherwise; especially when these same scientists have written books on the subjects putting their names and reputations on the line.

What has happened is not restricted solely to the scientific world but reflects what has also happened to the world at large. Scientists, cherished institutions, businesses and others in positions of power today are more concerned with money, prestige and position regardless of the truth as they disregard known errors in their theories and statements. In other words today's leaders, today's experts and others in positions of power are putting that same money and power before the truth. In the end the whole works is corrupted as they back each other up, knowing if one falls they all fall therefore they all hang together and vehemently deny the truth even in the face of undeniable proofs and facts, after all their reputations and salaries are at stake while the ignorant unquestioning people are easily duped.

This is the true problem in society today; we have stopped asking about the motives behind studies, findings and end results not just in science but in everything the so-called experts tell us. We have become mindless, accepting sheep ready for the next shearing, ready to blindly believe what we are told. After all why would they lie to us? Duh, for the money, power and prestige!

People the world over have been indoctrinated to believe in the infallibility of scientists and other so-called experts when they pronounce their theories as facts, their opinions as the truth; and further they teach their false beliefs and ideas to new generations of children and the ignorant, believing masses; creating mindless yes-men incapable of reading between the lines and interpreting the known facts for themselves. In this way free thinking is curtailed.

TV, radio and the internet are all there with their trusted and expert opinions. Don't know something, instead of researching the truth and checking the facts simply look it up where someone is ready and waiting with their 'expert' advice; not sure what is happening in the world, simply check the sanitized news where you will learn everything they want you to know.

Unfortunately the rise in importance of greed, power and prestige over basic truth is not just with science and the scientists but also with the USA and further the world. The American people were known and admired the world over when we stood for what was right no matter the cost. This has drastically changed to where Americans are now distrusted the world over as today Americans are all about what's in it for me, what do I stand to gain. Americans have become synonymous with power and greed and it has spilled over into the rest of the world while Americans themselves have become distrusted even despised by the rest of the world. We as Americans need to get our own house in order; we need to get back to doing what is right no matter the cost not only just in science but in everything about our once great country. Only then can we move forward instead of sideways as we now are. Of course the right path is never easy but that never stopped true Americans before!

We need to question everything we are being told by the established institutions the powers that be because everything from their mouths is basically false as the so-called experts have become a power unto themselves intent only on keeping themselves in power no matter the cost in dollars or human lives.